ENERGIZING PEOPLE!

UNLEASHING THE POWER OF DISC

BY JUDY SUITER

Competitive Edge, Inc.
P.O. Box 2418 • Peachtree City, GA 30269
www.competitiveedgeinc.com

Energizing People: Unleashing the Power of DISC

Copyright 2003 by Judy Suiter
Published by Competitive Edge, Inc.

Design, illustrations and typography by Chris Carey
Photographs by Comstock and PhotoDisc

Cover photography: "Lighthouse at Sapelo Island, Georgia," by
Mike Sellers

Disclaimer: The purpose of this book is to provide insights
regarding motivation, personal improvement, and relationship
skills. It is not meant to replace professional counsel for legal or
financial matters, or for emotional or psychological issues.
Referral to a competent business consultant, or to a qualified
counselor or therapist, is recommended for use outside the scope
of this publication, which is intended for general use and not as a
specific course of treatment.

ISBN 0-9721790-0-3

Printed in U.S.A.
First Edition – June, 2003
Third Printing – March, 2004

Competitive Edge, Inc.
P.O. Box 2418 • Peachtree City, GA 30269
Office: (770) 487-6460 • Fax: (770) 487-2919
www.competitiveedgeinc.com
E-mail: judy@competitiveedgeinc.com
We accept Visa, MasterCard, and American Express

TABLE OF CONTENTS

DEDICATION

This book is dedicated to you:

- my readers
- my clients
- my suppliers
- my business associates
- my staff
- my family and friends

who have all been part of this lifelong journey of exploration into human behavior.

With appreciation
and affection,

Judy Suiter

ACKNOWLEDGMENTS

For years I have been doing presentations all over the world and have been continually asked if there was a book available that summarizes the DISC concepts for "normal" people. It is with great joy that this book has finally been completed. Contributions to the final product have come from many sources.

Very recently I had the opportunity to attend a seminar conducted by Dr. Phil McGraw, the behavioral scientist made popular through his association with Oprah Winfrey. Dr. Phil asked a number of thought provoking questions, one of which was, "Can you name the people who have been pivotal in your life?" Let me answer this question as the means of giving proper acknowledgement to those people who have helped me along the way.

First, I would like to thank Dennis Driscoll for introducing me to the DISC Behavioral Model, which changed my life and led to my becoming a Performax Systems International distributor in 1982. I decided to attend every certification program that was conducted in Atlanta, Georgia, in order to learn as much as I could from the trainers who were willing to share their time and expertise with me. I am very grateful to Ann Minton, Lew Russell, Bob Picha, George Glover, Pamela Cole, and the late Anneliese Dilworth for giving me the basic foundation of my DISC knowledge.

In August, 1982, I was on a shuttle bus going to the hotel where the Performax National Convention was being held when I was fortunate to make the acquaintance of the late Dr. Ralph Morel and his wife Bertha. Both of these caring individuals became not only lifelong friends but business mentors as well. During the convention, they introduced me to Dr. Michael O'Connor, who is one of the top behavioral and organizational consultants in the world. Through his mentorship over the next four years, Dr. O'Connor provided me with the knowledge to move my application of the DISC model to a whole new level and showed me how the values systems of people impact their behavior. To this day, he continues to be a knowledge resource for my professional growth and a valued personal friend.

At that same convention, I was introduced to Bill Bonnstetter, who was a training coordinator for Performax Systems International at that time. Bill later became the founder and CEO of Target Training International, Ltd. In 1989, Bill offered me the opportunity to become a distributor of the TTI Performance Systems computer-generated *Managing for Success*™ DISC behavioral reports. This defining event facilitated a reciprocal collaboration between our two companies to validate and develop tool sets that have allowed trainers and consultants to provide greater insights to their clients all over the world.

In the early 1990s, I was in San Juan, Puerto Rico, on business, and through happenstance, I met Dr. David Warburton, Professor of Human Psychopharmacology at the University of Reading, in the United Kingdom. He is the founder of ARISE (Associates for Research Into the Science of Enjoyment), an organization devoted to studying the positive contributions of pleasure to health and everyday life. Dr. Warburton, Bill Bonnstetter and I combined our talents and interests to provide the first Content, Construct and Validity Study for TTI Performance Systems in 1992. David continues to provide research assistance, support, and friendship, but most importantly, he continues to push me to always ask the critical questions with regard to research and design.

I would be remiss if I did not recognize a few additional people who were instrumental in getting this book into this final form. First is Earl Suttle, who has constantly badgered me to "just get it done." Next is my research team, Janet Boyce, Chris Carey, and Lucy Lea, who helped in the writing, formatting, proofing, and editing of this book; my office staff, Darbie Bufford, Lynn (Iggy) Kahl, and Carol Schug, who provided daily support for my business and put up with my increasing levels of stress.

And last, but not least, my two sons, Brett and Drew, who endured constant hours of being my "guinea pigs" in bringing this knowledge to life.

INTRODUCTION

Throughout the ages, philosophers, military leaders, doctors, and psychologists—among others—have tried to fit human behavior into a model that includes predictive qualities.

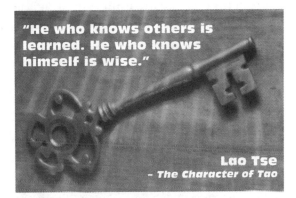

"He who knows others is learned. He who knows himself is wise."

Lao Tse
- The Character of Tao

Many centuries ago, Hippocrates recognized four different temperaments that he identified as *Choleric, Sanguine, Phlegmatic,* and *Melancholic.* Why did he feel a need to classify people and/or groups of people into these four descriptions of behavior? He thought he could predict the outcomes of wars by understanding the behavioral characteristics of the warring factions. Over the centuries, Hippocrates's original concepts and theories have been modified, researched, and redefined to create more current, useful models. These are being employed in a variety of ways, including career counseling, conflict management, job matching, succession planning, team building, and stress reduction.

The value of being able to *predict* our actions and the reactions of other people under different sets of circumstances allows us to have a greater sense of control over our own lives, leading to a more optimistic viewpoint. Current research shows us that the more optimism people possess, the stronger their immune systems becomes, resulting in healthier human beings. In our ever-changing world, understanding the behavior of ourselves and others—especially under stressful circumstances—enables us to have a corner of sanity in a world of chaos.

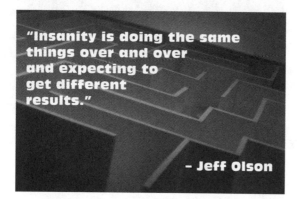

"Insanity is doing the same things over and over and expecting to get different results."

– Jeff Olson

We can learn a lot about optimism by looking at certain sports figures. A wonderful story is told by a man who played a round of golf with Sam Snead, one of the world's greatest golfers. Sam posted a seven on the first hole of their game, three strokes over par. Yet he seemed unconcerned. His only reaction was, "That's why we play eighteen holes of golf." It was important to him to keep his cool and not give up. Snead won their match, finishing four strokes under par. That's how optimism pays off!

Pat O'Brien, the former CBS sports commentator, discussed certain sports figures who had taught him great lessons about life. He praised Michael Jordan as a great athlete who never let a mistake hold him back. Once Jordan missed seven shots in a row, but he "never hesitated a moment to shoot the eighth." Jordan simply said to himself, "I know I'm not terrible. I just have to keep shooting until I hit one."

The power of positive thinking, of being optimistic, often is the difference between a winner and a loser. Do you recall ever hearing that Michael Jordan was too ill to play a game of basketball? Never. Being optimistic has many rewards.

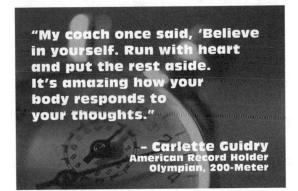

"My coach once said, 'Believe in yourself. Run with heart and put the rest aside. It's amazing how your body responds to your thoughts."

– Carlette Guidry
American Record Holder
Olympian, 200-Meter

Nowadays, it is crucial for all individuals to know as much about themselves as others know about them.

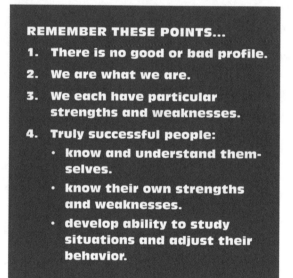

"To be successful in business today, it's not enough to be talented, to have great technical skills. You must master the art of interpersonal relationships."

– Judy Suiter

How well people understand themselves and how they best utilize their talents can mean the difference between success and failure.

REMEMBER THESE POINTS...

1. There is no good or bad profile.

2. We are what we are.

3. We each have particular strengths and weaknesses.

4. Truly successful people:
   - know and understand themselves.
   - know their own strengths and weaknesses.
   - develop ability to study situations and adjust their behavior.

This book is my attempt to discuss in layman's terms a model of human behavior, developed by Dr. William Moulton Marston, commonly referred to as DISC. I believe knowing and applying this information—putting it to practical use—can have a positive impact on a person's life and relationships with others. I so firmly believe in the value of this model that I have been described as the "Apostle of DISC."

I hope that, by the time you finish reading this primer, you will have a clear understanding of:

- Yourself
- Others you work or live with
- Your own energy level
- How to reenergize yourself.

In other words, the time you invest in learning these skills won't just fill your mind with new ideas; it will fill your life with new possibilities for improved relationships in your personal and professional worlds.

WHAT IS THE POINT?

People are different in their preferences, their viewpoints, and their behaviors. This statement does not presume that differing behavioral styles are good or bad, better or worse—they are simply different from each other. The way we see and respond to various situations identifies our behavioral styles.

For example, when people are faced with unexpected life challenges, they react differently: some fight for survival, while others retreat into denial by ignoring the problem. Still others turn to faith or join support groups. And some people thoroughly research and evaluate the situation to identify viable options before they take any action.

There are five basic truths regarding human behavior, and it's very important that you understand them:

- As people, we can observe the same situation yet perceive it in very different ways.

- Our perception is our reality.

- Most of us are more aware of our own behavioral strengths and values—and we are less aware of our limitations.

- While no set of behavioral traits or motivating values is better than others, the key is to understand our own style and values. Then we can adapt to different situations and environments more effectively.

- Adapting our behavior for different situations requires us to expend energy.

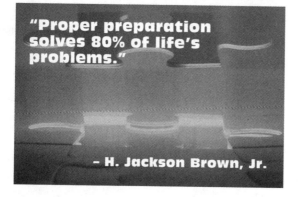

"Proper preparation solves 80% of life's problems."

– H. Jackson Brown, Jr.

WHAT DOES IT MEAN?

You and I have behavior-based preferences for interacting with others, who also have preferred ways for us to deal with them. This behavioral model is sometimes called a "doorway of communications" because, when someone deals with us in ways that are consistent with our behavioral style, we tend to "open the door" to them and their message.

Behavioral styles are composed of four tendencies that we call "D–I–S–C," an acronym that stands for:

D = Dominance, the need for control and challenging activities

I = Influence, the need to interact or persuade to our point of view

S = Steadiness, the need for security and stability

C = Compliance to high standards, the need for accuracy and cautiousness

---

The foundation of the DISC model rests largely on the work of William Moulton Marston, M.D., who, in 1928, published his behavioral research in the book *Emotions of Normal People*. Marston's purpose was not to put people in boxes or categories, but to provide a better understanding of their natural tendencies, strengths, potential limitations, and stressors.

The "DISC" Model provides a language to help identify how people:

- Handle problems and/or challenges (**D**)
- Interact and/or try to influence others (**I**)
- Pace themselves and handle change (**S**)
- React to rules set by others (**C**)

NOTE: Before we move on you, the reader, should know that there is a behavioral assessment available that incorporates one's responses to a profile and produces, via computer, a very personalized report that shows the magnitude of each of these tendencies (D, I, S, C) that one has. This report, known as Managing for Success™, is available for a small fee via the internet upon request. For further information about this profile, *turn to page 63 of this book.*

YOUR UNIQUE
BEHAVIORAL DESIGN

"We see the world not as it is, but as we are."

– Stephen Covey

Let's look at what it means to have "High" or "Low" tendencies in each of the four dimensions measured by DISC..

First, all people have at least some of all four tendencies—everyone has "**D**," "**I**," "**S**," and "**C**" traits. Each uses one, two, or even three of these behaviors more frequently than the other traits. We refer to this set of traits as an individual's *behavioral style*.

If we say someone has High "**D**" tendencies, we mean their "**D**" traits are above average, and Low "**D**" tendencies indicate their "**D**" traits are lower than average. "High" means above average and "Low" means below average. This is helpful in both describing and predicting your own and others' behavioral responses. To determine your style see the descriptions on the following page:

If you see yourself as *bold, daring, competitive, determined* and *direct*, you probably have *High* "**D**" tendencies as part of your style. On the other hand, if you consider yourself *cooperative, agreeable, humble*, and *indirect*, you most likely have *Low* "**D**" tendencies.

If *optimistic, inspiring, persuasive*, and *sociable* are adjectives that describe you, then *High* "**I**" tendencies are probably part of your uniqueness. Those with tendencies toward *objectivity, reflectiveness, aloofness*, and *distrust of others* have a *Low* "**I**" behavioral style.

Furthermore, individuals who are *adaptable, structured, patient, unhurried*, and *consistent* exhibit *High* "**S**" tendencies. Those with *Low* "**S**" tendencies are usually *hurried, excitable, flexible, intense*, and are often described as *dynamic*.

Likewise, those with a *High* "**C**" factor are driven to *perfection, precision*, and *accuracy*. They may be seen as *courteous* and *diplomatic*. However, adjectives such as *independent, unconventional, unstructured*, and *fearless* would fit the *Low* "**C**" individual style.

Now that you have a basic idea about these four tendencies, let's examine each factor in more detail.

D: *DOMINANCE*

The Dominance factor measures how you handle problems and challenges.

High "**D**"

- Tends to be very active and aggressive in gaining results
- Goes directly at any problem with little or no fear
- Usually relies on "gut" instincts

Low "**D**"

- Tends to approach a problem with a calculated, organized, well thought-out plan
- Tends to avoid conflict.

EXAMPLE: *Rudy Giuliani's behavior during the September 11th terrorists' attack on New York City is a good example of a person who exhibits High "D" tendencies. As soon as he heard the news, he immediately rushed to the crash site, compromising his own safety as debris and ash from the second collapsing tower rained down on him. Bold and daring actions were in evidence early in his public service career. He made a name for himself by promptly declaring war on "the mob" when he first became U.S. Assistant Attorney in 1983.*

ADDITIONAL "D" STYLE DESCRIPTORS

Recognize that the High "D" Style:

- Is results-oriented
- Has a desire to win
- Is a high risk-taker
- May be argumentative
- Listens for the key points and to important people
- Is quick to challenge

Recognize that the Low "D" Style:

- Approaches problems cautiously
- Is slower paced
- Has little need to challenge or lead
- Is slow to anger
- Tends to listen well

If you want to get a person with High "D" behavioral tendencies to do something, just say, "I bet you can't!" Their natural response will be, "You're on!" If you say, "I bet you can't," to people with Low "D" behavioral tendencies, their natural response will be, "You're probably right."

▮: *INFLUENCING*

The Influencing factor measures how you interact with other people.

High "▮"

- Tends to have high contact ability, outgoing and social
- Very persuasive verbally
- Tends to trust others and be very optimistic

Low "▮"

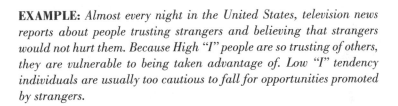

- Tends to be more sincere and reserved
- Approaches situations and relationships cautiously

EXAMPLE: *Almost every night in the United States, television news reports about people trusting strangers and believing that strangers would not hurt them. Because High "I" people are so trusting of others, they are vulnerable to being taken advantage of. Low "I" tendency individuals are usually too cautious to fall for opportunities promoted by strangers.*

ADDITIONAL "I" STYLE DESCRIPTORS

Recognize that the High "I" Style:
- Is a creative problem solver
- Is enthusiastic
- Uses humor
- Is fun-loving and impulsive
- Is a great networker
- Has never met a stranger

Recognize that the Low "I" Style:
- Is cautious in relationships
- Is usually distrusting
- Is a data-gatherer
- Prefers written documentation
- Makes decisions on facts, not emotion

I tell my audiences that High "I" people have never failed at anything, but they have had many significant "learning experiences." It's said they don't understand things until they experience them, while Low "I" people tend to avoid experiencing things until they understand them.

S: *STEADINESS*

The Steadiness factor measures how you handle a steady pace and change.

*High "***S***"*

- Tends to prefer a more structured, predictable environment
- Prefers having the "pond" clearly defined
- Desires and seeks secure situations

*Low "***S***"*

- Tends to prefer an unstructured, undefined environment
- Prefers to have a great deal of freedom to operate

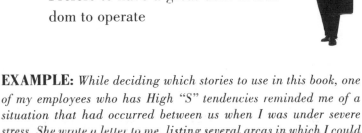

EXAMPLE: *While deciding which stories to use in this book, one of my employees who has High "S" tendencies reminded me of a situation that had occurred between us when I was under severe stress. She wrote a letter to me, listing several areas in which I could improve my management skills and reduce my stress levels.*

This story demonstrates my assistant's High "S" tendency to avoid verbal confrontation by writing out her concerns and providing written documentation for me. In her letter, she reinforced multiple times that she hoped I understood that her intentions were only to help me. If I implemented her suggestions, the end result would be a work environment where she would feel more comfortable. Several weeks later we found ourselves laughing about this situation.

ADDITIONAL "**S**" STYLE DESCRIPTORS

*Recognize that the High "**S**" Style:*

- Requires closure
- Needs security
- Is the best listener
- Can calm and stabilize others
- Is a good short-term planner
- Is able to mask emotions
- Has more patience than other styles

*Recognize that the Low "**S**" Style:*

- Needs little structure
- Works at a fast pace
- Shows emotion
- Is good at multi-tasking
- Does not enjoy tasks that require sequential thinking or repetition

Because they tend to feel guilty when they must turn down a request for help, a good motto for High "**S**" types  to practice is, "What part of NO don't you understand?" Because High "**S**" types are much slower paced, a motto Low "**S**" types prefer is, "What part of NOW don't you understand?"

C: *COMPLIANCE*

The Compliance factor measures how you respond to rules and procedures set by others.

*High "**C**"*

- Tends to follow rules set by others, including grammar and spelling rules
- Is very aware of the effects of failing to comply with rules and procedures
- Is extremely cautious

*Low "**C**"*

- Tends to do it "my way" or "pushes the envelope."
- Establishes his/her own rules.

EXAMPLE: *Darbie, my executive assistant said she could hardly wait to tell me what had happened between her father and father-in-law, demonstrating the power of behavioral styles. During a family outing at a local mall, her very High "D" father-in-law "marched to his own drumbeat," walking fast, against the traffic flow. This drove Darbie's father crazy because of his High "C" tendencies. He kept repeating that they needed to walk on the other side. Her father-in-law continued walking very fast, and Darbie was afraid they were going to lose him, because he doesn't pay attention to little things. She told her father to just keep walking and try to keep up with her father-in-law, to which he replied that he didn't like going to the mall anymore!*

ADDITIONAL "**C**" STYLE DESCRIPTORS

Recognize that the *High* "**C**" Style:

- Works well alone
- Has high expectations of self and others
- Is able to solve complex problems
- Organizes and analyzes
- Is self-competitive and follows rules
- May be overly critical of self and others

Recognize that the *Low* "**C**" Style:

- Will find a "new way" to do things
- May not see errors
- Thinks creatively
- Is open to change and new ideas
- Will go around rules

A High "**C**" believes if you're going to do something, do it right the first time, because you probably won't have time to do it over correctly. A Low "**C**" tends to believe it is both easier and better to beg forgiveness than get permission.

RECOGNIZING AND COMMUNICATING AMONG BEHAVIORAL STYLES

Although understanding yourself is important, recognizing, appreciating, and adapting to others is just as important for establishing and maintaining positive relationships.

Whether at work, or at home, or in social situations, the ability to tolerate differences among people and not take things so personally enriches our interactions.

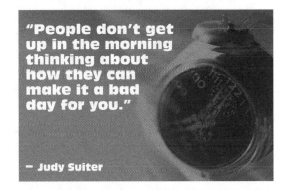

"People don't get up in the morning thinking about how they can make it a bad day for you."

— Judy Suiter

Knowing and applying DISC information cannot guarantee that everything will go smoothly with everyone, every time, but there are specific strategies for what to do and what *not* to do as we relate to each style. Recognizing the clues will help you build on your own strengths as well as those of your co-workers and family members.

People interpret your meaning and motivations— they even judge your integrity—by passing observations about you through the filter of their own behavioral style. Most of the time, they don't understand they even *have* a behavioral style, so this isn't a conscious process. As you might expect, people are more likely to judge you favorably when your style "agrees" with or is similar to their style. Of course, the less your styles agree, the less likely they are to see you in a positive light.

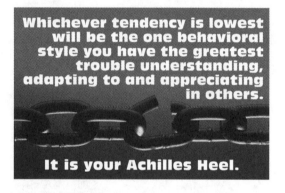

Whichever tendency is lowest will be the one behavioral style you have the greatest trouble understanding, adapting to and appreciating in others.

It is your Achilles Heel.

Communication, which is the focus of this chapter, is both verbal and physical. Socrates wrote, "People believe what you *do* before they believe what you *say.*" It's important that words and actions agree so our communication will create understanding and trust. The words we choose in communicating with each style can be very important in reaching understanding. Some *words* are turn-offs while others are turn-ons, so let's look at how to say what we mean. Likewise, certain *actions* are turn-offs for a particular style, while others are turn-ons.

To reinforce the value of choosing the best words to communicate with a particular style of person, let me share this story about Secretary of State Colin Powell.

A number of years ago, I provided training for FORSCOM Headquarters, where then-General Powell was the facilities commander. Two of his speech writers attended my program on DISC. By using the "people-reading" process, the entire class agreed that General Powell had a "C/D" style. Suddenly, one of his speech writers jumped up, turned to his co-worker, and pointed excitedly to that person's behavioral style graphs. He exclaimed, "This is why *you* never get red marks on the speeches *you* write for General Powell!"

He had just realized that his colleague's behavioral style was very similar to General Powell's, while his own style was very different. Because he filtered information differently, he was always getting "red marks"—the General's corrections—on his speeches. His colleague's work was more naturally agreeable to the General's style.

Because it is difficult to interact with individuals whose tendencies are significantly different from your own, the following clues will help you understand and communicate in a more effective way. These factors are most recognizable in identifying turn-ons and turn-offs for each behavioral style. While the *lows* are just as important as the highs, we are going to focus on the *highs* for each factor over the next few pages.

THE HIGH "D" FACTOR:

Primary Fear: Being taken advantage of

Turn Ons: (Energizers/Satisfiers)

- Challenges
- Leadership opportunities
- Tough assignments
- Options
- Decision-making and problem-solving

Turn Offs: (Dissatisfiers)

- Mundane or repetitive work
- No authority
- No challenge

Words/Phrases to use with High "**D**" styles:

- Win
- Results
- Leader/Leadership position
- Be the best (or be the first)
- Challenge
- Bottom line benefits
- Fast, immediate, now, today, new and unique
- Let's rock 'n roll

D "When the going gets tough, the tough get going!"

THE HIGH "I" FACTOR:

Primary Fear: Social rejection or not being liked

Turn Ons: (Energizers/Satisfiers)
- People interaction
- Social recognition
- Situations requiring enthusiasm/energy
- Spontaneity
- Positive reinforcement

Turn Offs: (Dissatisfiers)
- Being ignored or overlooked
- Skepticism
- Negativity/pessimism

Powerful Words/Phrases to use with High "I" styles:
- Fun
- I feel
- Exciting
- You will look great!
- You should earn an award for…
- Lots of people
- Picture this….
- "I am pumped!"

"There are no strangers in my life, only friends I haven't met yet."

THE HIGH "S" FACTOR:

Primary Fear: Loss of stability and security; confrontation

Turn Ons : (Energizers/Satisfiers)

- Security
- Closure
- Team harmony
- Defined territories
- Helping others

Turn Offs: (Dissatisfiers)

- Loss of security
- Lack of closure/completion
- No space to call "my own"

Words/Phrases to use with High "**S**" styles:

- Think about it
- Take your time
- Can you help me?
- Trust me
- Our history shows that…
- Promise
- Security
- Our reputation for service

"You can do anything you want to do if you stick to it long enough."

THE HIGH "C" FACTOR:

Primary Fear: Criticism of their work or efforts

Turn Ons: (Energizers/Satisfiers)

- Information
- Quality standards and rules
- Organizations that value rules
- Analysis/research
- Time for reflection

Turn Offs: (Dissatisfiers)

- Unwarranted personal criticism
- Irrational feelings/emotions
- Unscheduled or risky changes

Words/Phrases to use with High "**C**" styles:

- Here are the facts
- Proven
- Guarantees
- The data shows
- No risk
- Analyze
- Supporting data
- Just let me know…

C "I know I have faults, but being wrong is not one of them."

NOW WHAT?

As you absorb this information, you'll see how it can be used in a variety of ways, especially when working with people outside your normal team or group.

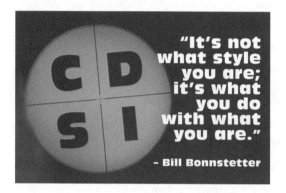

"It's not what style you are; it's what you do with what you are."

— Bill Bonnstetter

The DISC behavioral model is extremely useful when dealing with current and/or potential customers. Regardless of our job descriptions, we all "sell" products, services, or ideas in our work or personal lives. At the very least, you and I must continually sell ourselves—our credibility, reliability, and viewpoint—to others.

As with all information, DISC insights will do you no good if you only know them but don't use them! The more you practice, the better you will become in assessing others correctly. You will gain skill in thinking and working strategically, applying these concepts to reach your full potential and build more fulfilling relationships both professionally and personally. As my friend Lucy Lea has observed, "It's not just a *work* thing; it's a *life* thing!"

HANDLING CHANGE AND ENERGY DRAINS

Change is more than a challenge—some people become charged up by it, while others become paralyzed. Regardless of what people think of change, it is truly one of the few constants we have. If we stay in one situation long enough, it will change, just like the weather!

As you might expect, each behavioral style has a predictable and distinctly different approach or reaction in dealing with change:

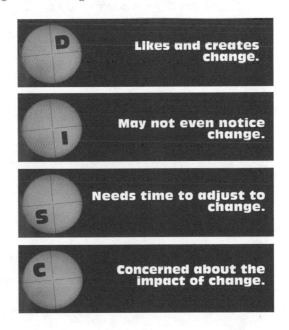

STRESS AND CHANGE

Every behavioral style requires energy to effectively manage personal and professional life changes. When people experience stress, pressure or fatigue, they do not have energy to adapt their behavior. Therefore, they attempt to compensate by overextending (and abusing) their greatest strengths. In today's business climate, stressful change is continual—and sometimes drastic—from one day to the next. Here are predictable reactions under stress:

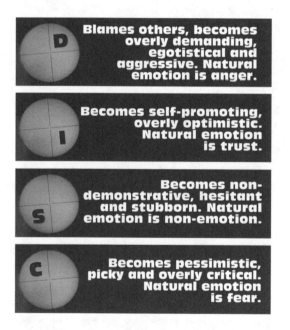

As they say, the only stress-free people are dead! However, when people know their own style and can recognize another person's style, they can make choices about how to interact with that person. For your own good health, it is necessary that you take time to understand and meet your individual needs for care and attention. And, since you are gaining knowledge about how each style reacts to stress, you will also recognize methods for facilitating change that create more positive and productive responses from each style. Making wise choices leads to a greater sense of control and optimism regarding expected outcomes and lowers stress levels for everyone.

Research shows that no bodily function is immune from the effects of stressful thoughts, emotions and behaviors. How you think affects your cholesterol level, blood count, stomach acids, immune function, and level of endorphins (the body's natural pain-relieving chemicals).

Tom Laughlin, addressing the effects of stress and imbalance in our lives, writes that every illness, no matter how slight, should cause us to ask the following question:

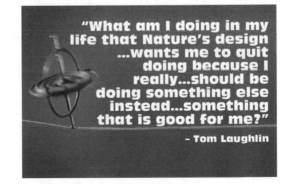

"What am I doing in my life that Nature's design ...wants me to quit doing because I really...should be doing something else instead...something that is good for me?"

– Tom Laughlin

HIGH "D" STRESS INDUCERS

- No results achieved, or lack of challenge
- Poor use of time and resources
- Mundane, repetitive tasks
- Stupid mistakes
- Being told to lower their voice

HIGH "I" STRESS INDUCERS

- Routine, regimented schedules
- No one to talk to
- No fun or humor
- Spontaneity suppressed
- Conflict / confrontation

HIGH "S" STRESS INDUCERS

- Being forced to make unexpected changes
- Having to redo tasks
- Experiencing discord within workplace or home
- Nonproductive time-wasters
- Having their personal space invaded

HIGH "C" STRESS INDUCERS

- Chaotic or unpredictable situations
- Inaccuracies and mistakes
- People who violate rules and procedures
- Feeling inadequately prepared
- Dealing with overly emotional people

How do you deal with stress? One successful method is being aware of your own body's stress signals. Laughlin says your body sends signals that you should be doing something else that is good for you because it is more consistent with your true nature, what he calls "Nature's own individual blueprint." Keep attuned to your moods, emotions, and thoughts.

After a stressful experience, each behavioral style requires something different to recharge their batteries. Here are rechargers for each style:

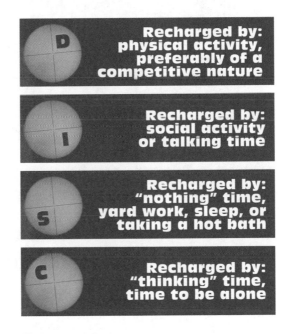

In effect, when you encounter stress caused by working outside of your natural design, you are required to use energy in adapting and adjusting your behavioral style to fit the situation. It's neither possible nor practical to operate only in your own comfort zone, so skill in adjusting is important to your success. The information in this chapter will help you understand the cause of energy drains and how you can reenergize yourself. As you put this information to work in your behavioral style, expect to see improvements in your physical health, energy, attitude and well-being.

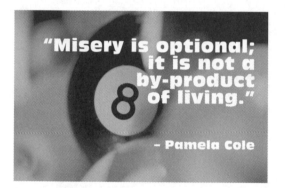

"Misery is optional; it is not a by-product of living."

– Pamela Cole

UNDERSTANDING ENERGY DRAINS

Use this information to recognize what types of environments, situations, and people have the highest potential to cause you stress or becoming an energy drain, so you can manage your energy more effectively. Relying significantly on your lowest traits and tendencies drains your energy most quickly. Remember, we refer to your lowest tendencies as your "Achilles Heel."

When people are stressed, they usually act to avoid their greatest fear, rather than living out of learned, conscious behavior. Ultimately, fear-based behavior leads to negative interactions and outcomes. The key is not to change your *natural* behavioral style but to equip yourself with strategies for *adapting* and *adjusting* your style appropriately. And you *can* do this—live consciously!

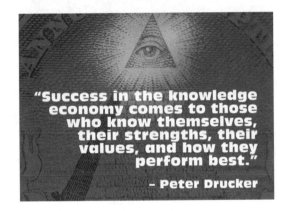

"Success in the knowledge economy comes to those who know themselves, their strengths, their values, and how they perform best."

– Peter Drucker

Change, stress, and energy drains are part of everyone's daily life. You will better understand how they work in yourself and others as you study these additional clues:

- how different behavioral styles process information
- how they learn new things
- how they make decisions
- how they measure their worth/value

Jim Rohn, "America's business philosopher,"

teaches how to master change and improve our lives. He says, "If you don't like where you are, change! You're not a tree. Those are not roots; they are legs. Move!"

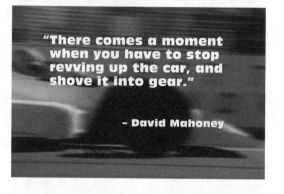

"There comes a moment when you have to stop revving up the car, and shove it into gear."

– David Mahoney

INFORMATION PROCESSING, DECISION MAKING, AND LEARNING STYLES

Since we have established that DISC acts as a filter for relating to our environment, it should be no surprise that your behavioral style provides your orientation for processing information and making decisions—even the ways you learn are influenced by your style. On the following pages, you'll find comparisons that show how each of these issues can be improved by understanding how DISC impacts them.

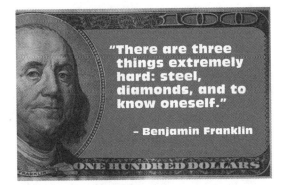

"There are three things extremely hard: steel, diamonds, and to know oneself."

– Benjamin Franklin

Individuals with High "**D**" behavioral styles tend to process information and make decisions based upon their "gut" feelings. The High "**D**" behavioral styles tend to learn best by discovering things for themselves, e.g., experiential training activities.

High "**I**" behavioral styles process information and make decisions by talking out loud and/or brainstorming with others. They may come to a conclusion after listening to themselves describe the problem to another person or by talking out loud. They learn best through discussion and audiovisual aids. "Say it and see it" works best for this group.

High "**S**" individuals process information and arrive at conclusions by logical analysis and a step-by-step process. They use pro-and-con lists regularly for making decisions. They learn best by reading information beforehand, observing the process, then doing the task while being monitored for accuracy. They prefer to have a reference manual available should questions arise. Flowcharts can also be very valuable to people with High "**S**" tendencies.

People with High "**C**" tendencies tend to process information by taking in all kinds of data simultaneously and then arriving at their decisions in a systematic, intuitive way. They learn best through visual examples/pictures and by facilitating learning for others.

HOW STYLES MEASURE THEIR OWN WORTH AND VALUE

People with High "**D**" tendencies tend to measure their value by the results they get and/or important positions and assignments they are given. Being named to a board of directors is a sure sign of success for someone with this style—it speaks of authority, power, and achievement.

High "**I**" tendency individuals measure their worth and value by the recognition they are given or awards they have earned. For example, a friend of mine has a bulletin board in his office with all kinds of memorabilia that continually reminds him of the acknowledgments he has been given over time.

Individuals with the High "**S**" behavioral style tend to judge their value and worth by the appreciation others show for their support and help. One way to enhance their personal value is by rewarding them with an extra personal day off or an unexpected bonus. They don't like a big show but appreciate acknowledgment.

High "**C**" individuals measure their personal worth and value by the increased levels of competency they achieve. An example would be mastering a new software program or attaining an additional college degree under challenging circumstances. Such achievements enhance their sense of self-worth.

DEALING WITH DIFFERENT STYLES

High "**D**" individuals want you to be efficient and give them options and/or probabilities for success up front. They need to feel they are in control, and the best way to do this is to offer them choices to make and tangible rewards to achieve. They want authority to do what is required to accomplish them.

High "**I**" individuals need stimulation and spontaneity; they avoid dull and repetitive tasks. They are influenced by testimonials and short-term incentives. They love recognition—if they give you a referral, send a small "thank you" gift. It's not the gift, but being remembered that matters.

High "**S**" individuals want amicable relationships. It is important to give them guarantees and assurances in writing, so they feel assured they can avoid conflict after agreeing. They are very practical and prefer to follow proven methods rather than trying new or experimental techniques.

High "**C**" individuals look for accuracy and quality assurances; they need to be provided with outstanding service and concrete evidence of quality standards. They are not swayed by emotional appeals or hearsay. Their personal standard is perfection, and they expect at least excellence from others.

EACH STYLE'S REACTION TO FEAR

When backed into a corner, High "**D**" styles fight to defend their positions. Recall President George W. Bush's stern, unemotional, and steely response to the September 11th attacks on the United States as he warned terrorists, "We will hunt you down; you will have nowhere left to hide in the world."

Emperor Justinian of the Byzantine Empire was a High "**I**," and when the Greeks revolted, he wanted to give up his throne and flee. His High "**D**" wife, Theodora, demanded that he stay and fight, resulting in his successful defense of his throne. He went on to become the most famous and admired leader of that empire.

High "**S**" types band together to increase their sense of security. Historically, resentment over lack of appreciation became the catalyst for unionization, hence the growth of unions during the industrialization period of the United States and the National Educators Association teachers union that exists strongly today.

High "**C**" types tend to withdraw in order to plan an attack strategy, or they may play mind games with others—they pride themselves on their critical thinking skills. Examples of world figures who were mind-game masters include Joseph Stalin, Bobby Fischer, General Irwin Rommel, and Nikita Khrushchev.

WHAT EACH STYLE NEEDS MOST TO LEARN

Each style has specific learning challenges and each needs to learn a specific trait.

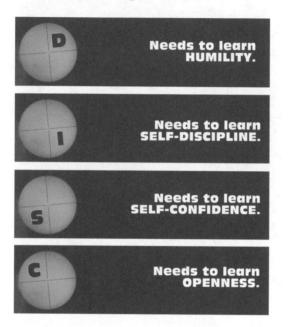

D — Needs to learn **HUMILITY.**

I — Needs to learn **SELF-DISCIPLINE.**

S — Needs to learn **SELF-CONFIDENCE.**

C — Needs to learn **OPENNESS.**

CULTURAL BIASES

If you are dealing with global organizations, look for clues as to the behavioral biases of the countries you visit. To recognize cultural biases of a country, consider their architecture, automobile designs, garden layouts, historical foundations, corporate structure, and how they interact with each other. Here are some examples:

In High "**D**" cultures, we see examples of pioneering spirit or entrepreneurship. In the past, you would normally have found a "top–down" hierarchal management model emphasizing authoritarian leadership. The U.S., South Africa and northern Germany are examples.

In Ireland, Italy and Portugal, expect High "**I**" to dominate the culture. This means they will reflect spontaneity—look for hugs and kisses, with lots of interaction. In such countries, you will find numerous open-air cafes, parks, and central meeting rooms that promote community and social interaction.

When you are visiting in Poland, Spain and Great Britain, you will notice that their culture bias is toward High "**S**." These countries reflect the importance of family, loyalty and tradition. For example, Great Britain still shows strong support for maintaining its monarchy. Another cultural clue is the high degree of organization seen in their gardens, with shrubs and flowers planted in rows.

The cultures of Sweden, Switzerland, and Japan reveal High "**C**" tendencies, which is why they are known for precision and high quality standards. In such cultures, you find a stoicness and a great emphasis on privacy. These can be seen in the secret Swiss bank accounts and the precision of Swiss watch making. Further evidence may be seen in the quality standards and processes adopted by the Japanese and Swedish automobile makers.

None of these examples suggest that the majority of people who live in these countries have the same behavioral style as their culture. Research conducted by TTI Performance Systems supports the contention that percentages of "**D**," "**I**," "**S**," and "**C**" styles are consistent around the world.

For instance, given a culture in which females are subservient to males, their adapted behavior in a mixed-gender group tends to be like a High "**S**." But, when the men are excluded and the women are in a group by themselves, the predictable traits of all four types are observed in expected ratios.

Think for a moment about the culture of the United States Marine Corps—everything you know about it screams High "**D**," and the environment attracts many "**D**" type soldiers. Yet, under the command of their leader, Marines learn to model "**C**" traits of precision warriors. The behavior of a Marine is modified by his environment, so even a High "**D**" recruit will follow orders to the letter and comply with rules and regulations. But removed from that environment when he is discharged from military service, you will quickly see evidence of his natural style.

One of the most valuable insights you should gain from this information is "When in Rome, do as the Romans!" Issues of style even influence cultural attitudes toward tipping restaurant workers or negotiating the price of a souvenir. In one country, these may be expected, while in another country, they are considered inappropriate.

Adapting and adjusting is the key to fitting in. "**D**" type behavior may be acceptable in a culture that has a bias toward those tendencies. But it may be highly offensive in another culture where teamwork or compliance is a dominant value. The same is true of unadjusted "**I**," "**S**," and "**C**" behaviors, too. How we process information and reach decisions requires us to be aware of cultural biases.

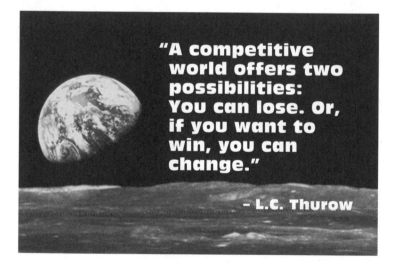

"A competitive world offers two possibilities: You can lose. Or, if you want to win, you can change."

– L.C. Thurow

MAKING SENSE
OF IT ALL...

Now that we have these insights about ourselves and others, what do we do with them? The answer is DO SOMETHING!

Feedback from readers of the previous edition suggests that multiple readings of this book will reveal the power of this information. I encourage you to share this information with others, both at work and at home. As you share and discuss these concepts, you will gain additional understanding and rewards.

Take a few minutes to remind yourself how powerful you truly are and how much you will enhance your personal power when you combine it with the power of DISC!

Remember that "effectiveness is always a matter of choice, not chance." Choose to discover and develop your full potential!

At Competitive Edge, we hope you have found this book interesting and helpful. Through our office and web site, we offer a variety of resources to help you apply this information for your personal and professional growth. Abraham Maslow said, "When the only tool you have is a hammer, you tend to treat every problem as a nail." Our goal is to provide you with the tools you need to build a successful life.

Earlier, I mentioned the *Managing For Success*® style assessment, which individuals can access on the Internet and complete in their home or office. We also provide assessment and consultation services for departments and companies, to assist their recruitment, retention, and motivation efforts. And our "train the trainer" conferences equip clients to relay the content of Competitive Edge Seminars most effectively to their employees.

Please contact our office to:

- order additional copies of this book
- obtain our other books
- complete your own *Managing For Success*™ style assessment
- explore our consulting services
- receive further training

Thank you for reading—now go do something great with this life-changing information!

Work like you don't need the money. Love like you've never been hurt. And dance like no one is watching!

LAGNIAPPE

In southern Louisiana, *lagniappe* means a little something extra, a token gift a shopkeeper might include with a favorite customer's purchase. Here is a list of some of my favorite web sites as a *lagniappe* for you:

www.arise.org — understanding the positive contributions of pleasure in everyday life, founded by Associates for Research into the Science of Enjoyment.

www.askeric.org — a free online question and answer service.

www.askjeeves.com — a more interactive search engine and database, it contains detailed answers to all manner of questions.

www.audiotech.com — summaries of business books, briefings, CDs and cassettes.

www.businessbriefings.com — this site selects and weighs big ideas from 327 magazines, journals, newsletters and websites–the Idea Bank–then adds its own unique analyses, insights, and forecasts.

www.chriscarey.com — a source of thoughtful information for "solving your people puzzles" by one of my associates, you'll find motivational wallpaper for your computer and even an online magic trick with a powerful life lesson.

www.ask.elibrary.com — newspaper and magazine articles from all over the world, plus large archive library.

www.fastcompany.com — founder Mark Agee says, "when you're a small company with limited resources and you are dealing with 800-pound gorillas, you have to look at the world a little differently."

www.ml2.com — their motto is, "Making a Life, Making a Living: Reclaiming your purpose and passion in business and in life," founded by Dr. Mark Albion.

www.nurturemarketing.com — make your customers call you when they are ready to buy! Founded by James P. Cecil. I recommend *The Cure For The Common Cold* booklet.

www.redwinereviews.com — choose the wines you will drink for dinner. Ten top Cabernets, Merlots, Pinot Noirs, Zinfandels, Shiraz and Meritages. Founded by Drew and Karen Suiter.

www.super-solutions.com — Success Performance Solutions web site, founded by Ira S. Wolfe. Great newsletters and archived information!

www.tourbus.com — a "Click & Clack" web site founded by Bob Rankin and Patrick Crispen, it will help you become web savvy. As they say, "Most people don't pay attention to the calm voice of reason, unless it's juxtaposed by screaming idiots on either side of the fence."

ABOUT THE AUTHOR

"Dynamic, supercharged, a walking encyclopedia, compassionate with an emphasis on passion—a passion for work, for people and for life in general." These are words used by a friend to describe Judy Suiter, whose company's motto, "Be daring, be first, be different," is also her personal credo.

Judy is founder and president of Competitive Edge, Inc., located in Peachtree City, GA since 1981. She started her company with only $58.38 in cash; today, Competitive Edge is recognized internationally as a top human resources training and consulting company specializing in candidate selection, team building, sales training, executive coaching and professional speaking.

She is a graduate of Middle Tennessee State University with a degree in Industrial and Personnel Psychology. She has over 440 hours of advanced study in behavioral sciences and organizational development.

Judy is also the author of *Exploring Values—Releasing the Power of Attitudes,* based on Eduard Spranger's research on the six motivating values. She also wrote *The Ripple Effect—How the Global Model of Endorsement Opens Doors to Success.* With Bill Bonnstetter and Randy Widrick, she is co-author of *The Universal Language— DISC Reference Manual,* currently in its 9th printing.

Judy has two grown sons, enjoys travel and golf, and is known by many as a gourmet cook. She also believes in giving back to her community. For the past three years she has served as a mentor for the Georgia 100 Mentor Program. Judy is a member of the American Business Women's Association, having twice been selected as the Business Associate of the Year. She was Woman of the Year for 1997, and is past president of ABWA's McIntosh Chapter.

In 2000 and again in 2001, *Women Looking Ahead* news magazine selected Judy as one of the "100 Most Powerful and Influential Women Business Owners in Georgia." She also serves as an advisor in the Chairman's Club for one of her key suppliers, TTI Performance Systems, Ltd. Because she is willing to share both her knowledge and herself with others, Judy Suiter is recognized as a role model and a leader in business.

Judy's writing associate for this book is Chris Carey, president of CreativeCommunication in Atlanta, Georgia. He is the author of several books about "solving people puzzles," including *Getting to Know You* and *The Price and the Prize.* Among hundreds of thousands of business consultants worldwide, he is one of 10 hon-ored as "Guru of the Year" by Guru, Inc. Chris is a professional member of the National Speakers Association, and in his platform career, he has presented his motivational concepts to more than five million people.

A CLOSING THOUGHT

I have searched diligently yet unsuccessfully for the source of this essay. I conclude many of my seminars with these words and share them to encourage you to include and involve all types of people in your life.

People come into your life for a reason, a season or a lifetime. When you figure out which it is, you know exactly what to do. When someone is in your life for a reason, it is usually to meet a need you have expressed outwardly or inwardly. They have come to assist you through a difficulty, to provide you with guidance and support, to aid you physically, emotionally, or spiritually. They may seem like a godsend, and they are. They are there for the reason you need them to be. Then, without any wrongdoing on your part or at an inconvenient time, this person will say or do something to bring the relationship to an end.

Sometimes they die. Sometimes they walk away.

Sometimes they act up or out and force you to take a stand. What we must realize is that our need has been met, our desire fulfilled; their work is done. The prayer you sent up has been answered, and it is now time to move on. Next!

When people come into your life for a season, it is because your turn has come to share, grow or learn. They may bring you an experience of peace or make you laugh. They may teach you something you have never done. They usually give you an unbelievable amount of joy. Believe it! It is real! But, only for a season.

Lifetime relationships teach you lifetime lessons, those things you must build upon in order to have a solid emotional foundation. Your job is to accept the lesson and love the people anyway; put what you have learned to use in all other relationships and areas of your life. It is said that love is blind, but friendship is clairvoyant.

Thank you for being part of my life.

— *Author Unknown*

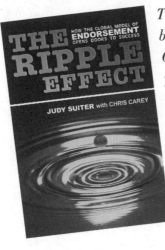

The Ripple Effect: How the Global Model of Endorsement Opens Doors to Success teaches you how to build strong networks of support through increased influence and credibility. The principles of endorsement are at work all around us, and Judy shows you how to recognize and cultivate them. This book reveals

- Sources and resources of endorsement—what endorsement provides for people, organizations, and nations
- Five elements that impact the level of endorsement enjoyed by people, organizations, and nations
- Five steps to improving your personal and professional endorsement
- Ways in which endorsement leads to improved performance through the Law of Reciprocity
- What causes loss of endorsement and how to regain it
- Specific methods for measuring and raising your level of endorsement

If you don't know what your values and priorities are, someone else will determine them for you! Just as *Energizing People* explains the "how" of human behavior, *Exploring Values—Releasing the Power of Attitudes,* reveals the "why" that motivates us to do what we do. This is the second book of Judy's trilogy and reveals

- How motivating attitudes and values are developed throughout life
- The six value clusters that have become the core for workplace incentive programs worldwide
- Well known individuals who demonstrate these values in action
- How to motivate others by understanding their attitudes and values
- Ways to appreciate and work more productively with people who have differing values clusters

The Ripple Effect: How the Global Model of Endorsement Opens Doors to Success and *Exploring Values—Releasing the Power of Attitudes* are available from Competitive Edge for $9.95 each, plus shipping and handling, or from the Associate from whom you purchased this book. Quantity discounts are available.

Managing for Success® is the computer-scored, online behavioral style assessment that unlocks the mystery of your natural and adapted styles by measuring the four factors of DISC. The report, over 20 pages in length, can be delivered to you via e-mail in PDF format, is compatible with any computer, and includes

- General and specific characteristics of your style
- Your value to the organization
- Dos and Don'ts for communicating
- Your ideal environment
- Self-perception and how others perceive you
- Keys to motivating and managing you
- Areas for personal and professional improvement

The applications for this information are unlimited and can be used for sales, customer service, team building, conflict resolution, interpersonal skills, management development, stress management, and marriage and family communication improvement.

Managing for Success® and *Personal Interests, Attitudes and Values* assessments are available online from Competitive Edge at a nominal cost, and group discounts are available.

Competitive Edge, Inc.
P.O. Box 2418 • Peachtree City, GA 30269
Office: (770) 487-6460 • Fax: (770) 487-2919
www.competitiveedgeinc.com
E-mail: judy@competitiveedgeinc.com

We accept Visa, MasterCard, and American Express